SEA RESCUE

EMERGENCY VEHICLES

Deborah Chancellor

This edition 2015

First published in 2012 by
Franklin Watts
338 Euston Road
London, NW1 3BH

Franklin Watts Australia
Level 17/207, Kent Street
Sydney, NSW 2000

A CIP catalogue record for this book
is available from the British Library

Dewey Classification: 623.8'887
ISBN: 978 1 4451 3816 9

Printed in China

Series editors: Adrian Cole/Amy Stephenson
Editor: Sarah Ridley
Art direction: Peter Scoulding
Designer: Steve Prosser
Picture researcher: Diana Morris

Franklin Watts is a division of
Hachette Children's Books,
an Hachette UK company.
www.hachette.co.uk

Picture credits:
B&J Photos/Alamy: 4.
Dave Booth/Alamy: 11.
David Brimm/Shutterstock: 16.
Paul Damen/Alamy: 7t.
Martin Fish/Lifeboat Photography: 6-7, 8, 10, 12, 13.
Neil Foster/Alamy: 9.
Jank1000/Dreamstime: 19.
Maritime & Coastguard Agency/AFP/Getty Images: 21.
Nortug: 20.
Steve Stone/istockphoto: front cover.
Nik Taylor Sport/Alamy: 5.
USCG: 14,15.
Bryn Williams/Alamy: 17.
YSSYguy/en.Wikipedia: 18-19.

Every attempt has been made to clear copyright.
Should there be any inadvertent omission,
please apply to the publisher for rectification.
Picture credits:

SPLOOSH!

Contents

Splash and dash

A Jet Ski splashes through the surf to save a swimmer. The lifeguard is wearing a wetsuit and a helmet.

AF-4814

SPLASSSH!

Bright colours make the Jet Ski easy to see in bad weather.

WHIRRRR!

A sled on the back carries a person back to shore.

Small and speedy

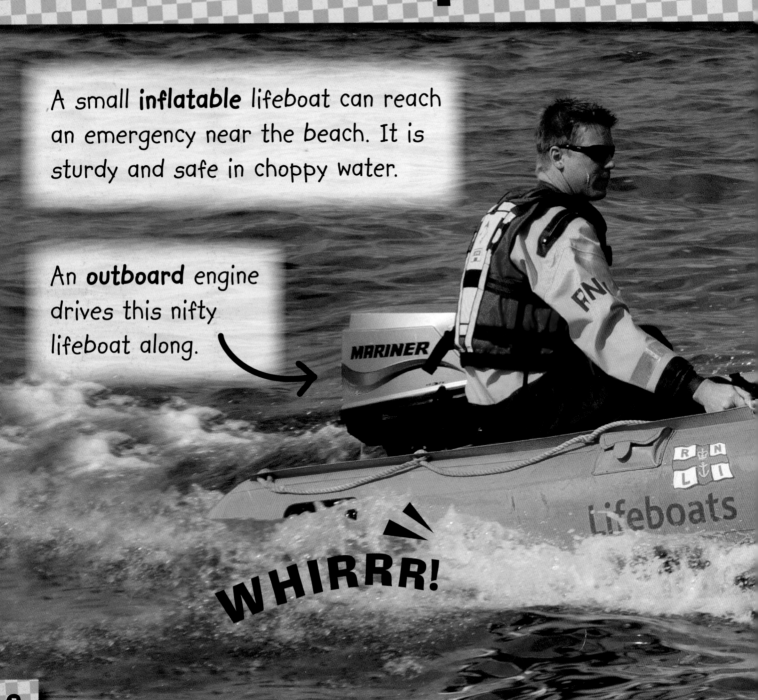

A small **inflatable** lifeboat can reach an emergency near the beach. It is sturdy and safe in choppy water.

An **outboard** engine drives this nifty lifeboat along.

MARINER

Lifeboats

WHIRRR!

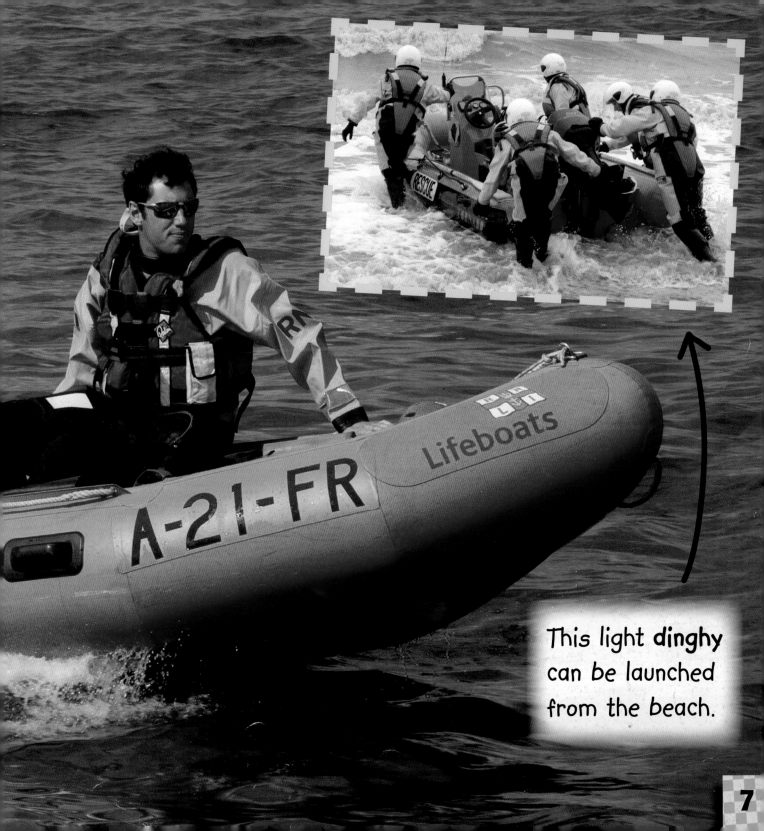

This light **dinghy** can be launched from the beach.

Ride the waves

This large inflatable lifeboat is built to survive rough weather.

Radar helps the crew to **navigate** by day and night.

SPLOOSH!

The crew wear safety belts to stop them falling out. Tough clothing and helmets help to keep them safe and dry.

BRRRMM!

SPLASSSH!

The lifeboat's **rudder** steers it in the right direction.

Air cushion

A rescue **hovercraft** zooms over water, mud and sand. It takes the quickest route to an emergency.

BRRRMM!

Two huge **turbines** thrust the hovercraft forward on a cushion of air.

WHHHRR!

Heavy weather

This all-weather lifeboat braves stormy waters to answer distress calls far out to sea.

Special equipment helps the crew with navigation and gives them the latest weather report.

CRAASSH!

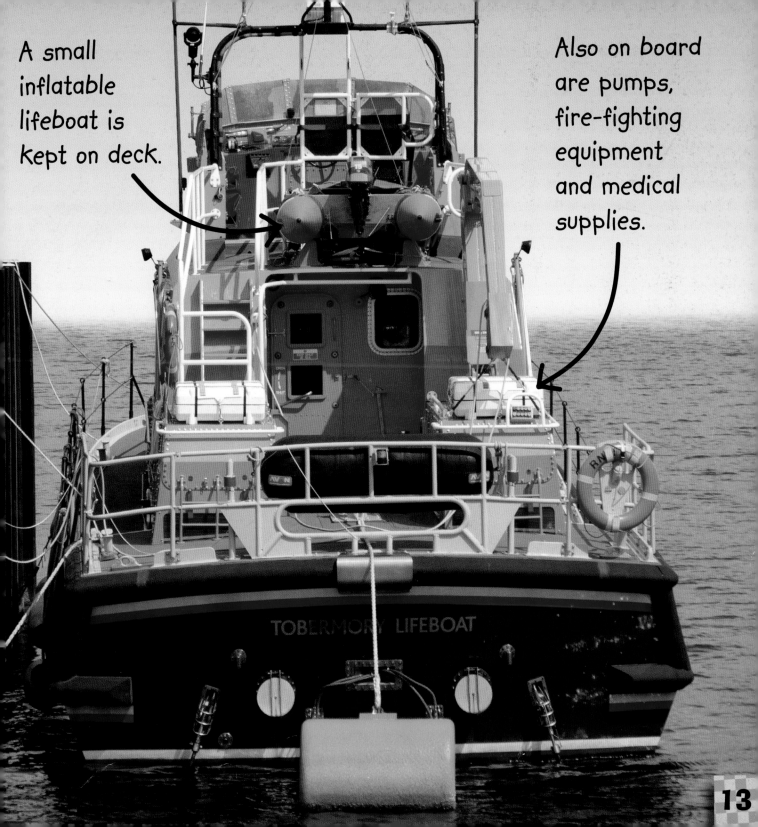

A small inflatable lifeboat is kept on deck.

Also on board are pumps, fire-fighting equipment and medical supplies.

TOBERMORY LIFEBOAT

High seas

This huge coastguard ship ploughs through the water to rescue the crew of a sinking boat. Navigation and radar systems are used to help with the ocean search.

U.S. COAST GUARD

913

A helicopter flies in to pick up a **survivor** and take them to hospital.

CHUPPA! WHUPPA!

The ship has a helicopter launch **pad** on the deck.

SWOOSH!

Over and out

CHUPPA!

WHUPPA!

Rescue helicopters can reach some emergencies more quickly than a boat.

Medical equipment is kept on board the helicopter.

A rescue helicopter lowers a safety line with a rescue worker to pick up people from the sea or from rocks.

Sky patrol

When disaster strikes at sea, planes drop rafts and other life-saving equipment to survivors in the water.

In some countries, search and rescue aircraft are **on call** 24 hours a day.

VROOOOOMM!

VROOOOOMM!

Rafts provide safety for survivors out at sea until more help arrives.

VH-PPJ

Tow away

This strong rescue tug is speeding to help a ship out at sea. Tugs can tow damaged ships, rescue survivors and fight fires.

BOOOOM!

NORDIC

These two rescue tugs are towing a container ship to safety.

CRAASHH!

There is space on board the tug for lots of survivors.

NORDIC
HAMBURG

Glossary

dinghy
a small boat

hovercraft
a craft that can move over land or water on a cushion of air

inflatable
something that can be pumped up with air or gas

launch pad
an area where a helicopter lands or takes off

navigate/navigation
finding the right way to go

on call
ready to set off for an emergency

outboard
placed on the outside of a boat

radar
equipment that finds out where another boat or plane is

rudder
a flat piece of wood or metal that steers a boat

survivor
someone who does not die in an accident or disaster

turbine
a motor that is driven by water or gas

Quiz

1. Why do rescue Jet Skis have sleds?

2. What kind of lifeboat can be launched from a beach?

3. How do lifeboats find their way to an accident?

4. Which sea rescue vehicle can travel over land?

5. How does a rescue helicopter pick up survivors from the sea?

6. What are rescue tugs used for?

Index

WHIRRR!